Knowing Constance Spry

A Comedy

Mary Rensten

A SAMUEL FRENCH ACTING EDITION

SAMUEL FRENCH

FOUNDED 1830

SAMUELFRENCH-LONDON.CO.UK
SAMUELFRENCH.COM

ISBN 978-0-573-03392-6

www.samuelfrench-london.co.uk

www.samuelfrench.com

FOR AMATEUR PRODUCTION ENQUIRIES

UNITED KINGDOM AND WORLD EXCLUDING NORTH AMERICA
plays@SamuelFrench-London.co.uk
020 7255 4302/01

Each title is subject to availability from Samuel French,

depending upon country of performance.

<h1 style="text-align:center">KNOWING CONSTANCE SPRY</h1>

First produced by the Cheshunt Dramatic Society in July 2002 with the following cast of characters:

Joyce	Pam Murphy
Victoria	Susan Murphy
Mrs Cowper-Jones	Barbara Mackay
Beryl	Michelle Fisher
Linda	Alison Rapley
Mrs Tipp	Pam Oswald

Directed by Brian Rapley

CHARACTERS

Joyce, in charge of teas at the Floral Art club, put-upon; 50s
Victoria, student, daughter of the new hall manager; 19
Mrs Cowper-Jones, a member of the Floral Art committee,
a would-be chairman, bossy; 50s
Beryl, at the beck and call of Mrs Cowper-Jones, very
unsophisticated; early 30s
Linda, the hall manager; 40s
Mrs Tipp, the projectionist, garrulous; 60-plus

The action takes place in a village hall

Time—the present

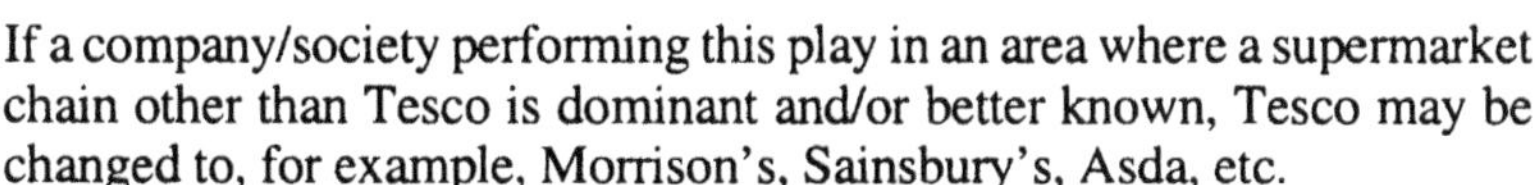

AUTHOR'S NOTE

If a company/society performing this play in an area where a supermarket chain other than Tesco is dominant and/or better known, Tesco may be changed to, for example, Morrison's, Sainsbury's, Asda, etc.

Also by Mary Rensten, published by Samuel French Ltd :

The Skip

KNOWING CONSTANCE SPRY

The interior of a village hall

We are looking at the wall at the far end. There are two exits, one DR *for all entrances to the hall, the other* UL *to the kitchen. Against the wall is a long table, the sort used for pasting wallpaper, but a bit stronger. On it is a shallow cardboard box from which a roll of polystyrene cups is sticking out at an angle. To one side of the table are two folding or stacking chairs*

After a few moments Joyce enters DR, *carrying an old-fashioned wicker-shopping basket over her arm. She wears an unexciting, floral print dress and flat sandals. On a good day she looks about fifty. Today is not a good day*

Joyce (*seeing the position of the table*) Oh dear. How am I supposed to serve the tea, if it's right up against the wall. (*She sighs, puts her basket down on the floor, lifts first one end of the table and then the other, gradually easing it away from the wall a couple of inches at a time*) And goodness knows where the projector will go.

Victoria enters UL. *She is nineteen, a student, and daughter of the new hall manager*

Victoria Oh, you shouldn't be doing that.
Joyce (*resting briefly*) Somebody's got to do it. (*She resumes lifting the table*)
Victoria Here, let me help.

Together they position the table about three feet from the back wall

How far d' you want it … ?

Joyce That's fine. Thank you. Just so long as I can get behind it. (*Letting out a breath*) Oh. Well now … (*Looking at the polystyrene cups*) Oh dear, no cups.

Victoria Yes, Mum says she's sorry about that, but it's the Bridge Club; they booked the Small Hall *and* the cups and saucers …

Joyce So I gather. Your mum, did you say?

Victoria Yes, she's just taken over as Hall Manager.

Joyce Oh. Right. Yes, of course, Mrs Poley. So you must be — Victoria, is that right?

Victoria Vicky.

Joyce Vicky. Right. And you're at university, doing — now somebody did tell me …

Victoria Design.

Joyce Design. Yes, of course. (*Looking around her rather desperately*) It's amazing what you can study nowadays.

Victoria It's very interesting.

Joyce (*not really listening*) Um. Oh. Yes, I'm sure it is. I'm sorry, Vicky, I really must get on.

Victoria I'll give you a hand.

Joyce Would you?

Victoria Yes, of course.

Joyce Oh, that's very kind. If you could get me a cloth for the table, that would be most helpful.

Victoria Sorry, I don't know where they're kept.

Joyce Left hand drawer, cupboard to the right of the sink.

Victoria (*moving to the exit* UL) Does it matter what colour?

Victoria exits UL *to the kitchen*

Joyce No. Oh no, anything will do, so long as it's cheerful. (*She takes a small dried flower table decoration out of her basket and puts it on a chair*)

Victoria enters with a pink cloth

Victoria This be all right? It's the best I could find; the Bridge Club have taken the gingham ones.

Joyce (*looking at the cloth doubtfully*) It's not quite what I'd like, but then neither is the table. (*She picks up the box of polystyrene cups and puts it on the floor*) Let's get it on.

Together they shake out the cloth and spread it over the table

Victoria Are you Mrs Jones?
Joyce Mrs Jones? No. I'm Joyce Barker.
Victoria Oh. I don't know where I got the name Jones from.
Joyce (*lifting the box of polystyrene cups on to the table*) We do have a Mrs Jones, well, Cowper-Jones. She wouldn't thank you for calling her Mrs Jones. (*She unwraps the polystyrene cups and starts to put them out on the table. They fall over*) Oh dear. This is not going to work. Oh, why do things have to be *so* difficult.
Victoria I'll get you a tray, Mrs Barker.
Joyce Oh no please, do call me Joyce. It makes me feel I'm not quite dead yet.
Victoria (*laughing*) OK. Joyce, then.

Victoria exits UL *to the kitchen*

Joyce continues to pull cups off the stack

Victoria enters with a tray

Victoria Here, this should do it. (*During the following, she sets out all the polystyrene cups on the tray and clears away the packaging into the box*)
Joyce It is a great nuisance, you know, having to serve the teas out here. (*She helps Victoria with the cups*) The whole point of having them in the Small Hall is that you can set everything out while the meeting's going on ——
Victoria — and miss the speaker.
Joyce What? Oh … yes. That's not always a bad thing. Thank you for doing this.
Victoria Don't you have anyone to help you?

Joyce Well. Yes and — no. (*She gets a bag of sugar from her basket*) It's very hard to get anybody, *anybody*, to volunteer these days. I'll just get a bowl for the sugar.

Joyce exits UL *to the kitchen*

(*Off*) It's not as if it's a complicated task, it's just … it's almost as if they think it's too menial.
Victoria What, serving tea?

Joyce enters with a bowl and teaspoons

Joyce Not the serving. Oh no, there are plenty of ladies who like to help with the serving. You can keep your hat on for that. (*She pours sugar into the bowl*)

Victoria, having cleared the packaging into the box, puts the box under the table

Victoria (*amazed*) They wear hats?
Joyce Well, no. I'm exaggerating, but metaphorically speaking they're wearing hats. You know, lady bountiful, look at me, aren't I being useful. One in particular, your Mrs Jones, always talking about how she once met Constance Spry.
Victoria Who's Constance Spry?
Joyce Oh, hasn't she come up in your course?
Victoria No.
Joyce Ah well, we are going back a bit there. She was a very famous flower-arranger, did the flowers for the Coronation in … oh, 1953.
Victoria Perhaps I'll get to her when we do gardens. No offence, but I'm not that keen on flower-arranging.
Joyce No, well … it is for older people … (*She gets a box of assorted biscuits from her basket and begins to open it*) Oh, what I would give to be your age again. How old are you — eighteen?
Victoria *Nine*teen. Nearly twenty.

Joyce It's still young. (*Struggling with the polywrapping on the box*) Oh, why do they make these things so difficult to open.

Victoria It's not all fun, you know, being young. There's exams — and assignments ... And men.

Joyce Men? More than one?

Victoria One is enough, thank you. (*Taking the box from Joyce*) Here, let me do that. It's not him so much. It's his mother, my ex-future mother-in-law.

Joyce (*taking a fancy plate from her basket*) Your ... What did you call her?

Victoria Ex-future mother-in-law. (*She has got the biscuits box open*)

Joyce Oh good, you've done it. (*She begins to put out biscuits*) I don't understand; you said your — mother-in-law?

Victoria Well, she would have been — if we'd got married.

Pause. Joyce stops putting out biscuits

Joyce Oh. So — what went wrong, if you don't mind my ...

Victoria Oh I don't mind. I'll tell the world. Now that it's too late.

As she listens, Joyce sets out the biscuits

The trouble was — I didn't say anything at the time. That was my mistake, I should have stood up to her. If I could have got him away from her, he would have been all right — my Peter.

Joyce Oh dear, I am sorry. What was the ... ? Was she ... ?

Victoria She hadn't chosen me. His mother. That's what it was, basically; her darling boy had thought for himself, for once. I ought to be running a mile from all this.

Joyce What do you mean?

Victoria Flowers, flower-arranging, floral ... whatever. She was a florist ... my ex — you know.

Joyce Oh. Oh, I see. (*She puts the empty biscuit box into her basket and puts the basket against the back wall*)

Victoria She had a shop. Polly's Plants. She was a bit like your lady; you know, the one with the hat. She once made a bouquet for Princess Margaret, and she never stopped talking about it. Anyway, enough of that, I'd really rather NOT think about her. (*Pause*) Joyce, listen … There are a few cups and saucers that have not been set aside for the Bridge Club, d' you want me to bring them in?

Joyce Oh no. That would create divisions, and we have quite enough of them already. I mean, who would have a beaker and who would have a cup?

Victoria Well, your lady with the hat for a start.

Joyce Oh yes, she would. By right.

Victoria By right?

Joyce Well … in her estimation, if no-one else's. She was a Miss Cowper, and way back her family had some position, I'm not sure what, but one of her ancestors did own a manor house, and I think some historical person slept there once.

Victoria Wow! Somebody famous?

Joyce I doubt it. If they had been I'm sure she would have told us. So, anyway … Miss Cowper … married Mr Jones ——

Victoria — and she didn't like her new name so she put the two together?

Joyce Exactly.

Victoria It wouldn't be the first time. I've got a friend called Ann Shoulder; she's just married a guy called Bone.

Joyce They surely haven't put their names together?

Victoria No, but everyone else has!

Joyce Who could resist it. Now … There are a few cups you said?

Victoria Yes.

Joyce Oh, I suppose we'd better have one for the speaker, and one for the chairman.

Victoria Not one for Mrs Cowper-Jones?

Joyce Oh, go on then. She'll only make a fuss if there isn't one, and it'll be my fault. (*She gets her dried flowers from the chair and places them on the table*)

Victoria You shouldn't let her sit on you, Joyce. I'm not going to let anyone sit on me again. I tell you, no way, not like she did, my ex.

Joyce Good for you. You should see the poor young woman that trails after Mrs Cowper-Jones, daughter of some woman who used to work for her at one time … Well that's the story. With Mrs Cowper-Jones, who knows? Beryl, she's called. I tell you, she needs to stand up for herself. (*Pause*) Well now … (*Brushing a couple of grains of sugar from the table, or some other finishing-off gesture*) That's all done I think. (*Looking at her watch*) Goodness, that didn't take long. I'm ever so grateful. I could almost go home and come back again. Yes, I could do that, I could switch the urn on now … It is filled, isn't it? I don't usually have to do that.

Victoria Yes, Mum did it this morning. Listen, you don't want to go home. Come with me to the pub,

Joyce The pub?

Victoria I'm sorry, do you not go to … ?

Joyce Oh course I do. I love pubs. I used to run one.

Victoria You … ?

Joyce With my husband. Oh yes. In London. In the City. We had all the bigwigs in there: lawyers, bankers, Lloyds names — I tell you, the wheeling and dealing that went on. You hear a lot when you're pulling pints. I'd love to come to the pub with you, Victoria.

Victoria Great. We can go through the kitchen, the back door's open.

Joyce and Victoria exit UL

Joyce (*as they go*) We had the Chancellor of the Exchequer in there once. He ordered a double whisky, I remember — and someone else paid.

Beat

After a few moments, Mrs Cowper-Jones' elaborate floral arrangement — a large bowl with high waving blooms and trailing ivy — enters DR *followed by Mrs Cowper-Jones' outstretched arms and finally Mrs Cowper-Jones herself sails in.*

She is bossy, in her fifties, and dressed in keeping with her floral arrangement — flamboyant hat and trailing scarves. She is in an excellent mood. Behind her comes Beryl, harassed, struggling with two loaded carrier bags and a slipping shoulder bag. Beryl is in her early thirties, very unsophisticated, and at the beck and call of Mrs Cowper-Jones

At the sight of the table, Mrs Cowper-Jones' mood instantly changes

Mrs Cowper-Jones Oh!!

Beryl stands stock-still. She knows better than to move, or speak

(*Shocked, appalled*) Who on earth has done this! Oh! (*Pause*) Beryl, take this, will you? (*Turning the bowl in Beryl's direction but keeping her eyes on the table*)
Beryl Yes — er yes, Mrs Cowper-Jones. Of — of course. (*She puts down one carrier but has trouble with the other, as the strap of her bag has fallen right down and become entangled with the carrier*)
Mrs Cowper-Jones Well, come along. (*Turning her head towards Beryl*) What *are* you doing?
Beryl (*extricating herself from the muddle and dumping the other carrier and her bag on the floor*) Sorry, Mrs Cowper-Jones. (*A weak smile*) It slipped — my bag.

Beryl takes the bowl from Mrs Cowper-Jones and puts it on the edge of the table. A trailing leaf is not quite right. Mrs Cowper-Jones sighs and adjusts it. Beryl picks up her bag. Mrs Cowper-Jones nearly steps on one of the carrier bags

Mrs Cowper-Jones Don't leave them on the floor. You do realize what's in that one, don't you?
Beryl Yes, Mrs Cowper-Jones — your biscuits.
Mrs Cowper-Jones Precisely. My biscuits. Beautifully crisp — and very delicate, as biscuits should be.

Beryl picks up the carriers and puts them on a chair

(*Surveying the table with distaste*) I cannot believe that anyone in our Society could arrange a table with such lack of taste. Just look at those … (*She indicates Joyce's dried flowers*) Do get rid of them.

Beryl (*taking them off the table*) Yes, Mrs Cowper-Jones. (*She places them tidily against a wall*)

Mrs Cowper-Jones (*the scorn in her voice could almost shrivel them*) And polystyrene beakers! Oh!

Beryl D'you want me to move them, too?

Mrs Cowper-Jones Do you seriously think I am going to drink my tea out of one of those?

Beryl No, I don't — but …

Mrs Cowper-Jones But what?

Beryl Well — if we were supposed to have cups and saucers, they would have been put out.

Mrs Cowper-Jones We always have cups and saucers. (*Waving her hand at the polystyrene beakers*) Oh, do get them off.

Beryl Couldn't you do that?

Mrs Cowper-Jones Pardon?

Beryl While I get the cups.

Mrs Cowper-Jones Oh, very well.

Beryl exits UL *to the kitchen*

Mrs Cowper-Jones begins collecting up the polystyrene cups and jamming them together

It's a good thing we got here early. As for this cloth — it'll have to do as a base I suppose. (*Calling*) Beryl?

Beryl appears in the doorway

Beryl Yes?

Mrs Cowper-Jones Why are we not having tea in the Small Hall?

Beryl (*who is expected to know*) I don't know.

Beryl exits

Mrs Cowper-Jones It's ridiculous; we can't possibly have tea in here. (*She puts the beakers on a chair*) Where are we to sit? And where's the projector to go? Mrs Tipp is not going to like this, she fusses at the best of times. Beryl, what are you doing?

Beryl (*off, calling*) I'm getting the cups.

Mrs Cowper-Jones Oh. (*Calling*) Don't bring them yet, I haven't put the cloth on. (*She goes to the carrier bags and from one she takes out an embroidered cloth with a lacy border. Humming, tunelessly, to herself she pushes aside the sugar. Still humming, she spreads her cloth so that one point hangs down, artistically, at the front. She places her flowers centrally on the lacy cloth, stops humming and stands back to admire her handiwork*) That's better. (*Calling*) You may bring the cups in now, Beryl.

No response

Beryl?

Beryl appears in the doorway

Beryl I don't think we are supposed to have them. There's a notice in here that says: "Bridge Club, Small Hall, cups, saucers and plates".

Mrs Cowper-Jones Oh don't pay any attention to that. It's probably an old notice.

Beryl Marjorie, it has today's date.

Mrs Cowper-Jones Please — I have asked you, not to call me that — not in public.

Beryl There's nobody here.

Mrs Cowper-Jones Not at this moment, no. But someone might walk in. Now, please bring the cups.

Beryl (*sighing*) Yes, Mrs Cowper-Jones.

Beryl exits and there is a loud clattering of china, off from the kitchen

Mrs Cowper-Jones (*calling*) And a large plate. Did you hear me?

Beryl (*off, shouting*) Yes, I heard you.

Mrs Cowper-Jones There's no need to shout, Beryl. (*She takes a Tupperware-type container from one of the carrier bags, opens it, takes out a home-made biscuit and nibbles it daintily*) Mmm ... (*Calling*) Beryl — what are you doing in there?

Beryl enters, carrying a tray with three cups and saucers

Beryl These are all I could find. There are a few mugs.

Mrs Cowper-Jones Mugs? No thank you. This is not good enough. Well, put them down.

Beryl takes the cups and saucers off the tray

I shall have to speak to someone. You've forgotten the plate.

Beryl Oh. Sorry.

Beryl scurries back into the kitchen

Mrs Cowper-Jones This is not the first time something like this has happened. If standards go on deteriorating like this I shall resign.

Beryl enters, holding a large plate, which she puts on the table

While Mrs Cowper-Jones is holding forth, Beryl arranges the biscuits, in a fancy pattern, on the plate

I have no wish to be associated with a second-class society. Of course, had I been Chairman, as I should have been, this would not have happened.

Beryl (*from whom a response is expected*) No. You're right; it wouldn't. It wouldn't have been allowed.

Mrs Cowper-Jones (*missing the sarcasm*) Exactly. I would have been Chairman, you know, had I not been on my Mediterranean cruise at the time. I was all for putting it off, you know ——

Beryl Yes, I do know.

Mrs Cowper-Jones — but Edgar insisted. He didn't realize what was at stake, of course ... but I knew, if I wasn't here — they would appoint someone else. (*Disbelievingly*) Elsie Catchpenny. Dear, oh dear. If the Club continues to go downhill we won't get the speakers. Not the best ones; they won't come. It soon gets around, you know, once an organization drops its standards. What *are* you doing with those biscuits?

Beryl Arranging them. Making them look — pretty.

Mrs Cowper-Jones Oh ... Beryl, they are biscuits, not flowers.

Beryl I know, but — you keep saying I don't try hard enough.

Mrs Cowper-Jones With your exhibits, no; you don't. They are always so — dull, your arrangements. No sparkle, no life. Which I find rather surprising.

Beryl I'm not a very — sparkly person.

Mrs Cowper-Jones My dear, I know that. But I did think by now some of *my* sparkle, *my* joie-de-vivre, *my* ... well, for want of a better word, my ...

Beryl Talent?

Mrs Cowper-Jones Well, yes ... indeed. I had hoped some of it might have rubbed off on you.

Beryl (*upset, in a small voice*) Well, it hasn't, and I don't think it ever will. (*Loudly*) And if you don't like the way I've arranged your precious biscuits, you can do them yourself.

Mrs Cowper-Jones Beryl — there's no occasion to be rude. Whatever would your poor mother have thought to hear you speaking to me like that.

Beryl (*gently*) I'm sorry. I wasn't being rude. I'm very grateful, but I am just a bit tired of hearing how — how very clever you are, how well-thought of and ——

Mrs Cowper-Jones Oh, my dear, I only tell you these things to encourage you. It's what your mother would have wanted, you know. (*Pause*) There is so much more you could do with your life, if you'd only ... well, let go a bit, be a bit more adventurous.

Beryl That's what I was trying to do. (*Pause*) With the biscuits.

Mrs Cowper-Jones Oh Beryl ... Thank goodness I brought my flowers. With such an eminent speaker coming. When I think how mortifying it would be if she were to have seen us decorating our tea table with those dreadful dried things … (*She moves her floral arrangement to the centre of the table*) There. What d' you think?

Beryl I——

Mrs Cowper-Jones No. To one side I think. More artistic that way. (*She moves them to one side and arranges the trailing ivy artistically*) Yes, that's it. Perfect. The finishing touch. (*She sighs*) Constance Spry herself couldn't have done better. *And* I grew them myself. (*Tenderly, to the plants*) Raised you all, didn't I?

Beryl raises her eyes to heaven

From tiny little plants. (*She turns to Beryl for approval*)

Beat

Beryl (*no emotion*) Yes, it's very beautiful.

Mrs Cowper-Jones smiles and with a tiny nod accepts the praise

But then — flowers are.

Mrs Cowper-Jones What do you mean: flowers are?

Beryl I mean — well, flowers are lovely in themselves. That's what my mother used to say. She said they don't need any tarting up.

Mrs Cowper-Jones Tarting up! Your mother would never have said that.

Beryl (*giving in*) It's a lovely arrangement. Almost like one of those bought ones.

Mrs Cowper-Jones flashes her an angry look

You're very clever.

Mrs Cowper-Jones (*graciously*) Thank you.

Mrs Tipp enters DR, *lugging an old-fashioned slide projector*

Mrs Tipp Oh no! No! Where'm I going to put my projector? Um? How'm I goin' to show your speaker's pretty pictures, Um? If I can't put up my projector?

Mrs Cowper-Jones It's no good asking me, Mrs Tipp. I have no idea where you are going to put your projector; I'm having quite enough trouble getting the tea organized.

Mrs Tipp No, well … You may not know, but somebody should've thought of it. Hallo, Beryl. You all right?

Beryl Yes, thanks.

Mrs Tipp You can't have pictures if you don't have a projector. I can't magic them for you. Not even my Harry could have done that, bless him. If you want pictures you're going to have to move your goodies from that table.

Mrs Cowper-Jones I shall do no such thing.

Mrs Tipp Your speaker's not going to be happy if I can't show her slides.

Mrs Cowper-Jones We shouldn't be here at all, we should be in the Small Hall for tea ——

Mrs Tipp   } *(together)* { Well, you're not …
Mrs Cowper-Jones   }   { —and we should be having cups.

Mrs Tipp … If you was, I wouldn't be fussing, would I? I'd be putting up my projector. I don't know who is responsible for this, but when I find them …

Linda enters UL

Linda I am responsible, Mrs Tipp, it's my fault.

Mrs Tipp Oh, it's you, is it? I wasn't to know that.

Mrs Cowper-Jones Your fault? Why, who are you?

Linda I'm Linda. Linda Poley.

Mrs Cowper-Jones I'm sorry, but the name means nothing to me.

Mrs Tipp She's the caretaker.

Linda I'm the new hall manager.

Mrs Tipp That's what I said.

Mrs Cowper-Jones Oh. Oh, I see. Yes, well then you are responsible.

Linda (*ruffled*) I said I was, and I'm sorry.

Mrs Cowper-Jones I am afraid sorry is not enough. We are *not* drinking our tea from ——

Mrs Tipp It's not the cups I want moving, it's the table.

Linda Look, Mrs Barker ——

Mrs Cowper-Jones } (*together*) {Mrs Barker!?
Linda } {— this is my first day and ——

Mrs Cowper-Jones I am not Mrs Barker.

Linda You're not Mrs Barker?

Mrs Cowper-Jones I most certainly am not.

Mrs Tipp That's Mrs Cowper-Jones, that is.

Linda Oh. Oh, I'm sorry. I thought it was Mrs Barker who did the Floral teas; I'm sure that's the name I had on my list.

Mrs Cowper-Jones It would be. You're quite right, it is Mrs Barker who does the teas.

Mrs Tipp Always done them, years and years.

Mrs Cowper-Jones I've just come along to add a few — finishing touches, you might say. (*Indicating her beautiful cloth and flowers*) The cloth and the décor are mine. Our speaker is a personal friend — and I know how much she appreciates a little artistry. (*She waits for the compliment*)

Linda (*not impressed*) Yes, it's very nice, but … Mrs Tipp's right. You'll have to move it. And those cups — they'll have to go back, the Bridge Club are using them.

Mrs Cowper-Jones (*enough of being charming to this caretaker woman*) They are not going back, we need them.

Linda I'm sorry, Mrs ——

Mrs Cowper-Jones (*precisely*) Cowper — Jones.

Mrs Tipp (*to Linda*) She was Cowper before she was married. Nice, putting the two names together, isn't it? And then Beryl here, her mum and Mrs Jones were ——

Mrs Cowper-Jones (*icily*) Thank you, Mrs Tipp. Mrs Poley does not need to know my history.

Mrs Tipp Oh, I wouldn't say that; caretaker needs to know what goes on. It's where everything happens, isn't it? Village Hall … weddings, parties, funeral teas.

Joyce and Victoria enter UL, *during the next speech. They wait by the kitchen door*

Linda Thank you Mrs Tipp. I'm sure, in time, I'll learn everything.

Mrs Tipp (*huffily*) I'm only trying to help. I'll come back later when you've sorted this out. And mind, I want to see that table moved. You don't move it, you don't get no pictures. When I took over this job from my Harry, bless him, he said I'd have to be firm with you ladies, and he was right. He wouldn't stand no nonsense, and I'm not going to neither.

Mrs Tipp exits DR

Mrs Cowper-Jones Oh, ridiculous woman. And so rude.

Linda I'm sorry, Mrs Cowper-Jones, but you will have to move the table, and as for the cups, the Bridge Club has booked them. And that was before I took over, so please, don't blame me.

Mrs Cowper-Jones But ——

Linda I can show you the order if you want.

Beryl I told her we couldn't have them.

Mrs Cowper-Jones Beryl dear, don't interfere. (*To Linda, as if speaking to a simpleton*) We always have cups and saucers; we do not have polystyrene beakers.

Linda (*patiently*) You cannot have them today. I'm sorry about it, but that's how it is. A lot of cups have got broken and I'm going to replace them as soon as I can, so that nobody has to have polystyrene beakers. But until I do, you'll have to manage. Where is Mrs Barker, anyway?

Joyce (*relaxed and a bit merry*) I'm here.

Linda Oh …

Joyce Your daughter and I … You are Mrs Poley, aren't you?

Linda Yes.

Joyce Victoria and I have been to the pub.

Mrs Cowper-Jones Really!

Joyce Oh, it's Mrs Cowper-Jones. Oh hallo, Beryl.

Beryl Hallo.

Joyce (*to Mrs Cowper-Jones*) What have you come for?

Mrs Cowper-Jones I beg your pardon?

Joyce To mess up my table by the look of it. What have you done to it?

Mrs Cowper-Jones You've been drinking.

Joyce It's what you do in a pub. And very nice it was too. I had a gin and tonic.

Victoria Two.

Joyce Yes. Two. I haven't had one of those for a very long time. Thank you, Victoria, it was a splendid idea of yours going to the pub.

Linda } *(together)* { *(appalled)* Vicky!
Victoria } *(together)* { *(to Joyce)* It was fun.

Joyce *(surveying her table)* Oh, look at that. Oh dear. Victoria, would you be a dear and take those cups and saucers back into the kitchen for me. We need them on the tray by the urn.

Victoria Yes, of course. *(She moves to the table)*

Mrs Cowper-Jones Just one minute, young lady.

Victoria What?

Mrs Cowper-Jones Don't you dare touch anything.

Victoria Yeah, but Joyce has just asked me ———

Mrs Cowper-Jones And *I* have asked you not to touch anything.

Victoria So?

Linda Vicky!

Victoria Let me tell you something, Mrs — Cowper-Jones. My mother is in charge here — OK? And unless there's something very wrong with my ears I distinctly heard her say you could not have the cups and saucers. *(She begins to collect up the crockery)*

Mrs Cowper-Jones This is an outrage.

Joyce I agree.

Mrs Cowper-Jones *(surprised, to put it mildly)* Oh. Thank you, Mrs Barker.

Joyce An absolute outrage. There are no other words for it.

Mrs Cowper-Jones I'm delighted to find you so in agreement with me. *(Addressing Linda and Victoria)* I come here, with one aim — to be of service.

Beryl has a sudden fit of "coughing"

Oh Beryl, do be quiet … I care about the Floral Club and I intend to see that our high standards are maintained.

Joyce (*applauding*) Well said, Mrs Cowper-Jones, well said.

Mrs Cowper-Jones Thank you. It's gratifying to have your support.

Joyce Oh, you have my support. Yes, oh yes. I don't mind bringing the odd flower or two ... I know they won't be in your class, that's not possible, but oh yes, I'm quite happy to help you make the table look nice; why not, we all want things to look nice ...

Mrs Cowper-Jones What are you talking about?

Joyce I should have thought it was obvious. You want the job of tea organizer — it's quite clear I'm not good enough. The job is yours. If you do all the preparation *and* you bring the flowers — well, you'll receive *all* the credit, won't you? So if you will excuse me, I will just take my — my poor dried flowers — a bit like me — and I will leave you to it.

Mrs Cowper-Jones Just ... Just a minute ... (*Strangely lost for words*) I — I ... Mrs Barker, please don't ... Beryl, help me.

Beryl Me? Oh no, this is between you two. I am staying out of it.

Joyce (*to Mrs Cowper-Jones*) This is what you want, isn't it? To be in charge, to tell everyone else what to do?

Mrs Cowper-Jones Not at all. No. I have no desire whatever to — to ...

Victoria To do the hard work.

Mrs Cowper-Jones I beg your pardon.

Victoria You just want other people, people like Joyce, to do all the grafting.

Linda Vicky!

Victoria Mum, I've met her sort before.

Linda Vicky, will you stop this!

Victoria No, Mum, I won't. This is something that has to be said.

Linda (*almost a whisper*) Yes, but you're not the person to say it.

Victoria Oh yes, I am. (*To Mrs Cowper-Jones*) You want Joyce to do all the work and then you come along, swanning in with your flowers ——

Beryl "coughs"

— making a great show, expecting all the praise.

Linda Vicky, for God's sake stop!

Victoria I am sure you are an excellent flower-arranger, but this is not about flower-arranging, Mrs Cowper-Jones — this is about people's feelings. (*Almost in tears*) You shouldn't tread on them.

Mrs Cowper-Jones You're very rude.

Victoria I'm just saying what's true.

Linda Vicky, that's enough. I'm sorry, Mrs Cowper-Jones, I do apologize for ——

Mrs Cowper-Jones If I've hurt anyone's feelings, I'm sorry, but I just cannot stand inefficiency.

Joyce It's all right Mrs Cowper-Jones — I'm not hurt. I think perhaps Victoria and I have had too much ... (*To Victoria*) We shouldn't have had that second drink.

Linda Come on, ladies, we must get this table moved. Time's getting on. Now, you decide which flower arrangement you are going to use — and I'll see if I can find you some cups.

Linda exits

Beat

Joyce (*to Mrs Cowper-Jones*) Yours, obviously.

Mrs Cowper-Jones Oh. Well, if you're sure, Mrs Barker, I wouldn't want you to think I didn't appreciate your ——

Joyce No no. Oh no, you've spent a lot of time on that arrangement, I can see.

Mrs Cowper-Jones Yes, well — it does take time, naturally ... I did spend most of the afternoon on it — but it's the skill that counts, you know ...

Beryl (*almost to herself*) And a little help from Tesco.

Joyce } (*together*) {Tesco?
Mrs Cowper-Jones } (*together*) {I beg your pardon! What did you say?

Beryl I said: you had a little help — from Tesco,

Mrs Cowper-Jones (*embarrassed, trying to laugh it off*) Tesco? What are you talking about?

Beryl I think Mrs Barker should know.

Mrs Cowper-Jones Oh Beryl, for goodness sake. Don't take any
notice of her, Mrs Barker.

They all wait for an explanation

Oh very well. What she is trying to tell you is, that … well,
sometimes, just very occasionally, I do buy just one, or possibly
two, of the flowers in my arrangements from the supermarket, but
that's only when my own blooms are not quite ready. I'm sure we
all do that from time to time. (*Brightly*) Now, let's get this table
moved: I wonder if we can do it without disturbing anything …

Beryl That's not what I meant. Nobody would mind just one flower;
it's when you go and do what ——

Mrs Cowper-Jones (*quickly*) Beryl, will you please be quiet. This
is not the kind of behaviour I expect from you. (*To the others*) Do
let's get this table moved. If Beryl and I take one end, d' you think
you could take the other, Mrs Barker?

Joyce Yes, of course.

Victoria   Don't you lift it, I'll do it.
                           } (*together*) {
Mrs Cowper-Jones   Come along, Beryl.

Beryl doesn't move

Beryl!

Beryl I don't like it when you — when you pass off something as
yours when it isn't. (*Pause*) You bought that arrangement,
Marjorie.

Mrs Cowper-Jones Oh, really! What a dreadful thing to say! As
if I would dream of doing ——

Beryl Oh I know you changed the bowl and added a bit of fern —
but it wasn't your arrangement and you did *not* spend the whole
afternoon working on it!

Beryl exits UL

Beat

Mrs Cowper-Jones (*to Joyce and Victoria*) She's very touchy, I'm afraid, on the subject of flower-arranging. I'm always winning prizes and I think she gets a bit jealous. It's very understandable; she's not had the opportunities that some of us have. Her mother, you know, was ——

Beryl enters

Beryl Sorry. I shouldn't have gone off like that. (*To Mrs Cowper-Jones*) I'll give you a hand with the table. (*She moves towards Mrs Cowper-Jones's end of the table*)
Mrs Cowper-Jones That was very hurtful, Beryl.
Beryl Yes, I know. I'm sorry.
Joyce (*hurriedly, dragging her end of the table to the back of the stage*) I think if we put it up against the wall, that will be all right. So long as Mrs Tipp has enough room for her project ——
Mrs Cowper-Jones (*letting Beryl move the table on her own*) Oh, that will be ample. It's going to be an awful nuisance for us, of course, but I suppose we'll have to manage. It's all very unsatisfactory.

Mrs Tipp enters DR

A little more this end, I think, Beryl.

Beryl moves her end

Mrs Tipp Oh no. No. You can't have it there. It'll have to go to one side. (*Indicating where she wants it*) If you move the chairs, you can put it over there.
Mrs Cowper-Jones Oh really, this is most inconvenient.
Mrs Tipp I agree, dear, very inconvenient. I should have had my projector up long before this.
Mrs Cowper-Jones I didn't mean it was inconvenient for ——
Mrs Tipp Oh, I know what you meant. Now come on, let's have it to one side.

Beryl I'll move the chairs.

Joyce starts to drag her end forward

Mrs Cowper-Jones Oh very well. (*Reluctantly and without any effort, she begins to move her end*)
Victoria No, wait a minute.

They pause

It makes no sense to do it like that. It needs to go the other way.
Mrs Cowper-Jones Which other way? There is no other way.
Victoria Yes, there is. It needs to be on the other side. Near the kitchen.
Joyce Why didn't I think of that? You're right, Victoria.
Mrs Cowper-Jones You had better check with Mrs Tipp first.
Mrs Tipp Oh, that'll be fine with me. Just right, that. Handy for the kitchen, and not in my way, neither. I'll just get me stand and I'll be back.

Mrs Tipp exits DR

Victoria Come on, then let's do it. Beryl, can you get hold of the other end?
Beryl Of course.
Victoria It's not heavy. I think we could lift it.

Together, they move it to UL, *leaving access to the back of the table from the kitchen exit*

Joyce Oh, thank you for that. (*Checking her watch*) Oh dear, just look at the time. Our members will be arriving any minute.
Mrs Cowper-Jones And our speaker. We don't want Mrs Hanford *to see us in this state of confusion; it gives quite the wrong* impression.
Victoria (*gasping*) Did you say Hanford?

Mrs Cowper-Jones Yes. I did.

Victoria Not — Barbara Hanford?

Mrs Cowper-Jones (*as if "who are you to doubt me"*) Yes.

Victoria Oh no, say it's not true. (*Furiously, to Joyce*) Why the hell didn't you tell me?

Joyce Tell you what? I don't know what you are talking about.

Victoria The speaker, for God's sake. Why didn't you tell me who it was?

Mrs Cowper-Jones I have just told you.

Beryl She doesn't mean you.

Joyce It didn't arise. I can't see what difference it ——

Victoria What difference?! She's only my ex-future mother-in-law!

Joyce No! Oh, Victoria. She can't be.

Victoria She bloody well is.

Mrs Cowper-Jones Mrs Hanford — your mother-in-law?

Victoria Ex. Future.

Mrs Cowper-Jones Pardon?

Victoria Oh my God, what am I going to do?

Joyce Well, that's easy. You're going to tell her what you think of her — aren't you?

Victoria What? Tell her what I think ... (*Her mouth going dry*) Oh, I couldn't do that — she'd tear me to pieces. Oh God, I'm getting out of here.

Joyce No, you're not. You're going to face her.

Victoria No.

Joyce Be polite. Just say *to* her all those things you said about her to me.

Victoria That was in the pub. I can't do it, Joyce.

Linda enters carrying a tray with an assortment of cups and saucers on it

Linda Here you are, ladies, I've found you some cups. Not that you'll be needing ——

Victoria Mum — it's her! The speaker! It's Mrs Hanford!

Linda I know, but ... What, not *that* Mrs Hanford?

Victoria Yes!

Linda I thought her name was Polly. This one's ——

Victoria No, Polly was for her flower shop. You know, Polly's Plants ... When she lectures she's Barbara.

Linda (*putting down the tray*) Yes, well, anyway, it's not really ...

Mrs Cowper-Jones Polly's Plants? What, that chain of shops? (*Scornfully*) Mrs Hanford doesn't run those. They're very ... well ...

Beryl Down-market.

Mrs Cowper-Jones Yes, I suppose that is the word.

Beryl   ⎫   ⎧ Not "top drawer" is what you'd say.
Linda   ⎬ (*together*) ⎨ Ladies, it doesn't matter ... .
Victoria   ⎭   ⎩ I'm getting out of here. Sorry, Joyce. I know what I said but ——

Joyce If you won't, I will. You spoke up for me, now it's my turn to speak up for you.

Linda Mrs Barker, I think you should know ——

Mrs Cowper-Jones (*overlapping*) I cannot believe that Barbara Hanford ... Those beautiful books she does ... I've seen her on the television.

Mrs Tipp enters with her projector stand

Linda (*shouting*) Ladies, will you please listen!

They are quiet

Thank you. (*Sighing*) Oh, nobody told me the job would be like this. (*Pause*) What I've been trying to tell you is — (*emphasizing each word*) — the speaker is not coming.

Mrs Cooper-Jones, Victoria, Beryl and Joyce all speak at once

Mrs Cowper-Jones (*simultaneously*) That's not possible, I've had a letter from her ...

Victoria (*simultaneously*) Thank God for that.

Beryl (*simultaneously, to Mrs Cowper-Jones*) You needn't have
    gone to Tesco's after all …
Joyce (*simultaneously*) We've still got to have tea.
Mrs Tipp (*starting a fraction after the others so we hear most of her
    speech*) Do you still want the projector, because if you don't you
    can put the table back where it was.

They all look at one another

Mrs Cowper-Jones (*to Linda*) What exactly did she say? I take it
    you have spoken to Mrs Hanford?
Linda No, I haven't spoken to her …
Mrs Cowper-Jones Then how do you know she isn't coming?
Linda I spoke to her secretary.
Mrs Cowper-Jones Oh. Oh, I see.
Linda And he said ——
Mrs Cowper-Jones He?
Linda (*trying to be patient*) Yes.
Victoria He's her boyfriend, I've met him.
Joyce I can't see it makes any difference, whether she has a male
    or a female secretary: the point is, she is not coming. Did the
    secretary say why?
Linda Yes, of course he did. If you'd let me get a word in. Her car
    has broken down — on the way here …
Mrs Cowper-Jones Oh, why didn't you say that in the first place?
    She'll be here, she'll just be late.
Beryl She's not hurt, is she?
Linda No, she's not hurt.
Beryl Oh, that's good.
Mrs Cowper-Jones Oh yes, it is good to know she's not hurt. So
    what time can we expect her?
Linda She is not coming. The car is not driveable, it has to be towed
    away.
Mrs Cowper-Jones Well, surely she could get a taxi. (*To Linda*)
    Didn't you suggest that?
Linda No, Mrs Cowper-Jones I did not ——

Mrs Cowper-Jones But why —— ?

Linda Because it's nothing to do with me; I simply took a message. And now, if you will allow me to, I'll tell you the rest of what the secretary said. (*Pause*) He said, Mrs Hanford was very sorry to let you down, and she would come and speak at the earliest opportunity and would your chairman please get in touch with her. All right?

Murmurs from the others

Now, do you still want these cups?

Joyce Thank you, yes, if would be nice; especially as you've taken the trouble to get them for us.

Mrs Cowper-Jones I am grateful to know she will be coming on some future occasion — but what about tonight? We have no speaker.

Beat

Beryl (*to Mrs Cowper-Jones*) You could do it.

Mrs Cowper-Jones Do what?

Beryl Give a talk.

Mrs Cowper-Jones A talk? I couldn't possibly do that.

Beryl You could, you know about flowers.

Mrs Cowper-Jones Yes, but ——

Mrs Tipp Oh go on, Mrs Jones. My Harry, bless him, he always said you had the gift of the gab.

Joyce I can't see why you're so reluctant; I thought you wanted to be the chairman.

Mrs Cowper-Jones I did. I do.

Joyce Well, Here's your chance.

Mrs Cowper-Jones It's not the same — chairing a meeting and giving a talk. I don't have any notes or ... No, I couldn't do it.

Beryl You could tell us how you do your arrangements.

Mrs Cowper-Jones What are you trying to do, Beryl, show me up in front of everyone?

Beryl No, I'm not, honestly I'm not. It's true, and you know it, that sometimes you … well, cheat a bit — and I did see you in Tesco's today … but most of the time they are yours, the arrangements — and they are very good — and I hate it because you know they're good *and* you say so. But, putting all that aside ——

Mrs Cowper-Jones I'm not sure I can.

Beryl Please, Marjorie. Talk about Constance Spry. You did actually meet her, didn't you?

Mrs Cowper-Jones Of course I met her. Are you suggesting that I —— ?

Beryl I'm not suggesting anything. If you say you met her, then ——

Mrs Cowper-Jones I did.

Beryl Well then …

Beat

Mrs Cowper-Jones I could, I suppose.

Beryl I'll help you.

Mrs Cowper-Jones You'll help me? What use could you be? You know nothing about floral art, you don't even like it.

Beryl That's only because you go on about it so much. I've learnt a lot from you. And I know all about Constance Spry.

Mrs Cowper-Jones Yes, well I do talk about her, I know that.

Mrs Tipp Are we going to have a meeting or are we not?

Joyce (*to Mrs Tipp*) I think we are.

Beryl That's not the only reason I know about her. My grandmother worked in her house.

Mrs Cowper-Jones Your grandmother worked … ? Your mother never said. *You* never said. Why did neither of you ever tell me? What did she do, your grandmother?

Beryl She was a maid.

Mrs Cowper-Jones Oh. Oh, I see. Even so, you should have told me. I am not a snob.

Mrs Tipp Come on, ladies, it's very nice to stand here being (*mispronouncing "philosophical"*) philosiful and all that, but you've got to make up your minds: are you having a meeting or are you not? And if so, do you want slides? Not that I've got any,

come to think of it.
Mrs Cowper-Jones } (*together*) No slides.
Beryl

They look at one another

Mrs Tipp No slides. (*She starts to pack up her projector*)

Beat

Mrs Cowper-Jones Miss Partridge and I ——
Victoria Who's Miss Partridge?
Mrs Cowper-Jones Beryl is Miss Partridge.
Victoria Oh. Right.
Mrs Cowper-Jones Miss Partridge and I will give a talk —— (*she looks at Beryl*)

Beryl nods

—— about Constance Spry. Her work. (*Query to Beryl*) And her life? Will you do her life?
Beryl Yes. I'll do that. And you can put your arrangement on the table in front of you.
Mrs Cowper-Jones Oh, but what about ——
Beryl Because we'll want, well, *you'll* want, to talk about it, being in her style, you know …
Mrs Cowper-Jones Oh. Yes, of course.
Beryl And Joyce's flowers — can go on the tea table!
Mrs Cowper-Jones Ah. Yes. Yes, indeed.
Joyce Much more in keeping — with the polystyrene cups.
Linda You won't need those; I'll get them out of your way.
Beryl The hall's filling up; we'd better go. (*Picking up the arrangement*) You carry it, it's yours.
Mrs Cowper-Jones (*taking it from her*) I do wish I hadn't gone to Tesco's.
Beryl It doesn't matter; nobody else knows.

Beryl and Mrs Cowper-Jones exit DR, Mrs Cowper-Jones squaring her shoulders and holding the arrangement in front of her, in the manner in which she carried it in

Mrs Cowper-Jones (*off*) Ladies, there is a slight change in the programme. Instead of your speaker being Mrs Barbara Hanford ——

Murmurs of regret

I am pleased to tell you that this evening we shall be hearing from someone who knew intimately — the great Constance Spry …

Murmurs of pleasure

Mrs Tipp If it's no slides it doesn't matter where your table is.

Mrs Tipp exits DR

Beat

Linda Oh, Vicky … why did I take on this job?
Victoria Because you like people, Mum — however odd they are.
Linda Hmmm.

Linda picks up the polystyrene cups and exits UL *to the kitchen*

Beat

Victoria I can't get over her coming here — my ex. It's too much of a coincidence. I bet she was coming to have a go at me.
Joyce She's involved with flowers and this is a Floral Art club. She was bound to come sooner or later.
Victoria It's the sort of thing she'd do, though. She'd like to show me up as "just the caretaker's daughter".
Joyce Hall manager's daughter.
Victoria Yes, that sounds better. I'm glad she didn't come. I couldn't have faced her. I tell you, I felt so weak and trembly when

I was having a go at Mrs Thing. Silly, isn't it?
Joyce No. It takes courage to be what you're not. Do you love Peter?
Victoria Yes. I do.
Joyce Then you'll have to talk to her sometime. Let me know when you're planning it, and we'll go to the pub first. A couple of doubles and we'll take her on together.

Victoria laughs

Come on, let's go and hear what Beryl has to say. If she can stand up for herself you certainly can.

They start to exit DR then Joyce turns back. Victoria waits for her

I nearly forgot. (*She retrieves her dried flowers from the chair, or under the table, and places them prominently on the tea table*) There. (*Pause*) I'll let you into a little secret, Vicky.
Victoria What?

Beat

Joyce They came from Tesco too.

CURTAIN

FURNITURE AND PROPERTY LIST

On stage: Long table. *On it*: cardboard box with stack of polystyrene beakers
2 folding or stacking chairs

Off-stage: Wicker shopping basket with dried flower arrangement, packet of sugar, packet of biscuits, fancy plate (**Joyce**)
Plain pink tablecloth (**Victoria**)
Empty tray (**Victoria**)
Sugar bowl and teaspoons (**Joyce**)
Large floral arrangement in the style of Constance Spry (**Mrs Cowper-Jones**)
2 carrier bags with Tupperware container of home-made biscuits, embroidered table-cloth (**Beryl**)
Tray with 3 matching cups and saucers (**Beryl**)
Large plate (**Beryl**)
Slide projector (**Mrs Tripp**)
Tray with assortment of cups and saucers (**Linda**)
Projector stand (**Mrs Tripp**)

Personal: **Joyce**: wrist-watch
Beryl: shoulder bag

LIGHTING PLOT

Property fittings required: nil

Interior. The same scene throughout

To open: Full general lighting

No cues

EFFECTS PLOT

Cue 1   **Beryl** exits to the kitchen. Pause   (Page 10)
Loud clattering of china from kitchen

Cue 2   **Mrs Cowper-Jones**: "... Mrs Barbara Hanford ——" (Page 29)
Murmurs of regret

Cue 3   **Mrs Cowper-Jones**: " ... the great Constance Spry ..." (Page 29)
Murmurs of pleasure

www.ingramcontent.com/pod-product-compliance
Ingram Content Group UK Ltd.
Pitfield, Milton Keynes, MK11 3LW, UK
UKHW021821150726
7214IPUK00017B/254